MEN'S DATING MAINTENANCE & REPAIR MANUAL

BECKY PARQUET

ISBN-10:0692605819
ISBN-13: 978-0692605813

DEDICATION

This book is dedicated to all those great guys out there
who have helped make my life much more interesting and challenging!

CONTENTS

PREFACE

This book is for men that are dating. Any references in here to your date being a 'her' can mean either a 'him' or a 'her,' depending on your gender dating preference. Hey, girlfriends or guy friends, feel free to give this to your potential man!

So, you're a man and you like to fix things? Great! A problem solver! Do you love the challenge of getting that lawnmower working again? Or better yet, hearing the roar of that car engine coming back to life after several hours of sweat and labor? Ah, yes: challenges! The staff of life. You guys are great at this! You can pick up your auto repair manual, read page 12, and there is the answer! Just a small part is needed. You order it, install it and VROOM!!!! You can almost taste the cold drink you will deserve after all of your hard work. Another challenge met. Just pick up the manual, find the right page, follow steps 1-6, and you're good to go!

You may ask yourself why dating can't be like that. Just pick up a manual, go to the relevant page and fix whatever is wrong. Well, it can be! Just because that old one didn't work, doesn't mean you're a failure. The steps are just a little different for repairing a relationship than for fixing a car. You just need to find the right manual for your particular make and model, and to look in the right place for the answers: inside this manual and inside yourself. Yes! You're an awesome guy with lots of potential. You just need to figure out how to make it work for you.

Just like when your car has problems, you can either take it to a shop (in this case, a therapist—and we all know how that goes over), or try to diagnose the problem yourself. Or both! If you decide to go the Do-It-Yourself route, you can have all the theories you'd like to on what you think will fix things, but if you don't have the experience or knowledge in order to know which 'parts' of yourself need fixing, nothing will work.

For example, let's say you're a big shot at a company or manage a sales team, and are \used to managing things but for some reason your stellar management skills aren't working with her? Well, a relationship isn't a company and your partner (or potential partner) is not the crew. It's a team, and you are one-half of that team. There's that 'other' person that needs to be taken into consideration. The lawnmower or the car engine might sort of sputter and die if you try the wrong thing, but I have yet to hear of one going off in a huff and slamming the door on its way out. Yikes! There are ways to avoid this as long as you know that-- *hey, you're not perfect* -- and you played a part at creating the broken motor in the relationship. You just need the skill and the willingness to meet the challenges of relationships that need maintenance or downright repair.

So, if you just pay attention, get over yourself, know what your goal is and want to meet the challenges, then you can attain that goal. Try to view problems, issues and tears as faulty spark plugs that need replacing or as leaking oil.

Please read ahead and, hopefully, you will find your own personal 'make and model.' You know who you are, guys. Have fun identifying the steps to repair your personal style, but be prepared to be honest with yourself and if you figure out that you are one of these, then pay attention! This in no way discounts any maintenance that must or could be performed on your significant other, but that's not your job, it's hers.

1 TOW TRUCK A

Broken hitch (aka divorced), baggage, commitment-phobic, etc.

PROBLEM:

Are you the guy that has been married and divorced and has not been able to find a committed relationship since? Maybe you've been a serial dater but each time it seems like something comes up that squashes any hopes you had that it would work. Are you clear on why your last relationship didn't work? Or are you clueless on why your ex left you? There was a reason. There honestly were things that led up to the breakup, but maybe you don't want to look at those reasons and think you'll just move on.

This new one, well . . . she talks so much, just like your ex. Or maybe she's a complainer or is too demanding! Just wait, any minute she will insist she choose your clothes for you, talking about settling down, and checking out baby clothes when you go shopping together. Yikes! Hey, this other one seemed just perfect, but then you found out she can't cook.

What is the deal? You're a great guy and go over once a week to help your ex. Well, she needed the help, right? And you know just how to repair that window. Or you have lunch together a couple times a week, and that *proves* you have no hard feelings and are not wearing your heart on your sleeve. You're overloaded with guilt about the divorce, so your kids always take priority, no matter what--even if you've made prior plans to take your new love on a test drive or to a movie.

Do you even realize the baggage you have loaded onto your car top carrier? Have you really let the past go and gotten over your ex? Are you used to having her in your life and find it hard to move on? Still secretly holding out hope you can't even admit to yourself? Is your new car complaining when you break dates for the ex because *"She has no one else to help her?"* Or have you had movie plans with your new date for two weeks and your ex calls you to take the kids because she wants her hair done, so you break your date? Sketchy boundaries spell trouble.

Has your resentment and bitterness over being "taken to the cleaners" clouded your view of the new cars entering your life? If you continue to compare and contrast your new cars to your old ex, this will never work! Just like your old car, your new car is an individual. She is not your ex. You are the one having trouble because you are putting her in the unfair position of having to justify her every action so that she won't be looked upon as a clone of your ex or of every bad dating horror story you've heard about.

Here is something to think about: She may not just be after your money. She may not end up being a backstabbing nagger as you thought your ex was. She may not hate sex. And it goes on and on. She is an individual and so are you. Can you just stop comparing? Get over that divorce, knock it off and move on. Whatever your ex was or wasn't like, that was her and that situation, and this is now. This could be a new and different beginning for you!

Hey, this new date also needs to see if you are right for her, just like you need to see if she is right for you. You are both separate cars with separate 'owners' in the past. Don't label her and bag her up ready to toss into the junkyard at the first sign of some similarity or fear she's going to imprison you! If you really want a good relationship, read on. If not, then enter the 'wants to date but nothing serious' on a dating website.

REPAIR STEPS:

❖ If you're seriously interested in finding a mate, then you may need to be seriously alone first. Think of that car as having gone to the junkyard and move on from that failed relationship or marriage. You're still a great guy even if you don't run to your ex's place every time she needs your help. She can find someone else to help her.

❖ Engage in activities you didn't do with your ex and go to places she won't go. Explore new car lots. Try doing things by yourself. Get to know who you are. If you make a date, keep it. Even if those wonderful kids want to see you the same day- if you made the appointment to see your new car first, see your kids on another day or time. They'll live and you will still be a good dad; they will see that you respect appointments and will be able to depend on you.

❖ When you take your new date out to a nice dinner and she appreciates it, please don't 'keep score' on how many times you've done this with her and how much it is costing you. Think of it as an investment into a happy, fulfilling life, with no expectations that if it doesn't work out with her, she will pay you back for all the dinners.

❖ If your new date buys you a sweater for Christmas, don't freak out and jump to the conclusion she is ready to get married and then not call her for two weeks. Thank her and go on to the next day.

❖ If a man looks admiringly at your date in the restaurant, don't take it as a signal she is ready to cheat on you. Let go of that car you traded in. She is not your ex.

❖ If your date asks you to meet her parents, it's a step. It's a nice step. It's another step. It's a different step towards getting to know who she is and how she was brought up, the dynamics of her family. It's ONLY a step. You're not signing the purchase agreement in ten minutes. And hey, when you meet the folks, wear that sweater she got you for Christmas!

❖ Enjoy the positive things about your new date. They may or not be similar to the positive things about your ex; but it is part of what makes up your new companion and adds to the relationship. Offer the positive things about yourself to her, as well. You have them or she wouldn't be with you.

❖ Be aware of when or if you are checking out your new date and are on high alert for 'red flags.' Sure, red flags do exist. Just make sure you're not looking for them around every corner. It's not fair. Have you ever been accused of just wanting sex? Same idea.

❖ So, she gave you 'The Look.' Ask her what she's thinking, rather than jump on the 'Oh no, that's just how MY EX used to look at me' bandwagon.

❖ When the new 'Ms. Right' shows up, you'll be ready. Her make and model AND her name will be unique.

2 RACE CAR

Goes too fast, all over the road, etc.

PROBLEM:

This has to be one of the most frustrating aspects of dating, when you think you've found 'the one.' You know what you want, right? She is...wow! You're a man and you don't let the grass grow once you know what you want. You make the decision and go after it.

The problem is she is not an 'it.' She has thoughts and feelings and would actually like to be part of the decision-making process. You say, *well, you know she's not perfect*, but so far, she's perfect for you. Why wait? You're so attracted to her and you're both grown-ups, after all. Or maybe you're both getting older--another reason to do the fast-track route.

Have you ever heard that women are like a slow oven? It takes time to warm them up. What exactly is your goal here? Okay, maybe you're serious and have a great goal. You want her in your life and you're sure. When she looks at you that certain way, to you it's THE signal to go full-speed ahead. Start kissing her soon because that's your rule. If she's a good kisser, it's on to the next step. Steer the conversation towards what you like to do in bed, does she like sex, what does she like, how often and all that leads to sex sooner rather than later. Make suggestive remarks every time you talk to her. That's the fast track. Yes, it is. The fast track to a dead end.

Have you ever tried this tact and been gently pushed away? Or worse, she gets angry and you end up feeling like a complete loser, like you've proven that *yes, you are only out for sex*. Just like 'every other' man she's known (she says.) But you're not just after that. Your behavior just makes it appear that way. 'If it looks like a duck.' Sure, sex is a big part of a great relationship, but the key word here is 'relationship.' This is not just about you and your needs. It's about an 'us.' In order to have an 'us' as your goal, then her needs must also be taken into account.

Just because she doesn't go as fast as you do, does not mean you can't ultimately achieve the same goal. The goal you were after in the beginning. Do you really want to be with her? Do you want to achieve this on your own with resistance all the way? Or do you want her to want it as much as you do? Do you realize how awesome that would feel? Patience is important and you can do this! It's your choice how you go about this. If you want her to burn out or her engine to quit, act like a racecar driver. If you want her to purr, treat her with care, warm her up gradually and pay attention to any sounds along the way that you may need to look into. In other words, slow down! If what you're saying or doing isn't being reciprocated, it's too soon. Patience, man.

REPAIR STEPS:

❖ Did you meet her online? Have you only written a couple of e-mails and seen her pictures? Continue acting like a gentleman. It will win points with her.

❖ Have you had a few dates and feel like just jumping into bed with her but you know she isn't ready? Continue acting like a gentleman. It will win points with her.

❖ Has she sent you a picture that attracts you and you haven't met yet? Have your thoughts. As many as you want. But keep them to yourself for now. Love that paint job but hold off grabbing the keys until you know how she runs.

❖ Is your brilliant idea to work your way into her sex life by starting to talk about it before you've even kissed her? Wrong.

❖ Maybe you've e-mailed, then talked on the phone and even Skyped. It's time, right? Perfect time to make suggestive comments about what you 'could' be doing after you meet, or how sexy she looks and what you'd like to do with that. Wrong.

❖ Take your time. Have conversations with her. Think about it like that vintage car you've been working on for months and what it will feel like to finally drive it. You can't rush it, right? It won't work until it's ready, but will it hum once it does! And I don't mean just sex. I'm talking about a relationship that hums in every way.

❖ You're trying an end-around tactic. You slip in little comments here and there that are boldly suggestive, then when she calls you out on it, you deny it! If she catches you grabbing the keys, be honest! Just tell her that's what was on your mind but you see that for her it's too soon, so it's fine to wait. Be honest and apologize to her if your little comments are offensive to her. An apology will go much further than a denial due to trying to sneak the comments in to see how she'd react.

❖ You can't get what you want from one, so you're branching out and trying many. You'll get your needs met from one of them, right? The odds are in your favor. Well, it all depends on what your goal is. Quantity or quality.

❖ Have you used excuses on her like, *We're both adults here*, or *We're getting older and don't have time to waste*, or (this is a good one), *We need to see if we're sexually compatible to know if this will work or not for the long-term*. Throw the 'LONG TERM' out there. This is also a good one: *My ex hasn't slept with me for years, I'm lonely and I hope you're not like that*. Go for the guilt, right? Use one excuse after another to get her on the fast track. These ideas will work great for a mile or so but not for a road trip. Drop them from your vocabulary.

❖ Again, this is about patience. Do you have it or don't you? You do if you practice slowing down and seeing the results, because you will see them. If the relationship starts to work in one way, it can snow ball and start branching off and working in many other ways, without crashing and burning. If that is what you're after, then please slow down or traffic tickets will start popping up all over the place.

3 REFRIGERATED TRAILER

Unaffectionate

PROBLEM:

Have you ever seen that old couple walking down the street, hand in hand? What were you thinking? Nothing? Blank stare? When she mentioned how sweet it was, you were at a loss for words because you weren't thinking at all?

This problem is almost the exact opposite from the Race Car. There is such a thing as too fast, yes. But too slow is equally as unfulfilling and will frustrate her (and ultimately, you) just as much. Again, what is your goal? Maybe you say you don't need affection, you didn't grow up on it, you've done fine up until now. You're not a touchy-feely man.

So, why does she look sad after the movie? The movie rocked! Full of action and all that other stuff (romance). Is your goal to be alone in a movie? Then go by yourself, guy! But if you are with someone you feel is wonderful and there's romance and tears in the movie, then engage her by reaching out and touching her to let her know you 'get it.' Or just look over and smile. She needs to know you're with her.

Affection isn't just about sex. It isn't just about hugging or touching. It is also about words and looks and feelings. Your smooth running relationship doesn't just depend on repairing problems when they come up. There has to be regular maintenance to prevent as many problems from happening as possible. Would you rather change the oil on a regular basis or spend tons of money and time replacing the engine. Over and over?

REPAIR STEPS:

❖ If you're driving and see a really nice ride next to you, how do you feel? Good, right? Look at situations where people seem to like holding hands and see if you can get a good feeling going. It can be a very touching part in a movie, (or if you see her people crying in the movie, that's your cue). Or maybe you're walking down the street with her, having a quiet conversation where you've both understood each other, etc.

❖ Look at her reaction when you hold her hand. Is it positive? Does she smile and squeeze your hand?

❖ Hugs are good. They are good for you physically and emotionally. Study situations and look at when others hug each other.

❖ Look at her reaction when you hug her. Is it positive? Does she smile or hug you back? Your maintenance is on the right track.

❖ Hugging and holding hands can also be part of the 'slow oven' thing she likes and needs. They are both very warm gestures and help both people feel closer. But affection isn't only physical. If she's sad about something, you can 'touch' her with affection by looking at her lovingly and telling her you understand.

❖ Pay attention to her cues. If she tends to hold your hand in certain situations, figure out what those are and next time reach out to her before she does. You will ROCK in her eyes.

❖ Everything isn't about sex. I know, a shocker! If you pay attention to her needs when there isn't sex, it does make the sex better when it happens. Keep the maintenance on track and it seriously lowers the need for repairs.

❖ You've both had a nice day and feel close and connected. Lie down and just hold her, without it leading to anything else. How does it feel? Remember what it feels like and enjoy it. It may be a challenge but it's a good one. There's a lot to be said for snuggling and just holding each other.

❖ Has lack of affection been a huge issue in your relationship? It's never too late to start. Start off slowly. Make just that one gesture and start off small. Get to a place where you are comfortable.

❖ Everyone is different and has different needs, but if you truly want to please her and make her feel special and lovable, giving her affection is a way to do that. It will help in all areas of the relationship. Be aware of how things may change in the relationship or how even you may change how you look at things once you start being affectionate.

4 LEMON

You've made a mess of your life

PROBLEM:

The divorce has been final for a long while now. You're living in a trailer. You quit your job, took Medicare early and the occasional drink has turned into a nightly event of self-pity. Life sucks, your ex took everything you had and is dating the personal trainer at the gym who, for all you know, was in the picture before the divorce. The alimony is sucking you dry and you see no light at the end of the tunnel.

It's been a long time now that you've been alone and you have no idea why. What happened? She just left one day and you have no clue as to why. You vaguely remember her getting angry a few times but then she would just clam up, and one day was just gone. You were the provider. You bought her everything she wanted, you watched while the credit cards bills piled up. But you cared for her, right? Sure, you were gone a lot for your job, but that's life, isn't it? She had a nice house, great clothes, even a housekeeper!

Can you see anything wrong with this picture? No? Is this what your life looks like, too? Believe it or not, things may not be as they seem to you now. Are you willing to take another look? A serious look at what may have really happened? I'm not saying this doesn't ever happen. It does! But in situations like this, just as in the rest of life, things may not always be as black and white as they appear. If this looks like your life, then your challenge, if you choose to accept it, is to get serious and realize that at every step of the way in your life, you had choices.

So, you say they can't be changed now. Nothing can be done to change the past. That's true, nothing can. But what you can do is change your present and your future, and make it into something much, much more fulfilling. I can't help you with how to find another job or another living situation, if that's what you want. But I do know that it isn't someone else's fault that you're where you are today in No-Relationship-Land. This is and has been your responsibility and you can take up the challenge to figure out how you got here and to avoid this happening in your future.

REPAIR STEPS:

❖ Go back to the beginning in your previous relationship or marriage and find the very first thing that didn't feel right. This might be hard, because you may not have seen it at the time. Then start making a list of what happened after that.

❖ She left without saying anything. Nothing at all? There appeared to be no reason at all that she would leave? Did you ask her? Maybe she didn't answer? Actually, what was the first thing you remember that didn't feel right? Did you have a conversation with her about that thing, or did you just go back to work?

❖ You always had choices in every previous situation you were in. What would have happened if you didn't decide to quit your job? Where would you be right now? Is it a profession you can return to?

❖ Were you working too many hours? You can fix that: try to find something that isn't so demanding. You probably know by now that being gone all the time can lead to being clueless when a relationship breaks apart. You both have to BE there in order to nurture the relationship.

❖ Are you on dating sites now and entering 'will not tolerate GOLD DIGGERS, anger issues or any baggage?' Seriously? And you don't have any at all? Enter things you like to do and don't start right off by advertising your own baggage!

❖ You've entered that you are 'retired' and that is what you say when talking with potential dates. But you know that you aren't. Get real. You quit your job because you gave up on life and now you're in a fog of self-denial. Start looking for a job that will be productive and fulfilling and when you meet someone, be honest with yourself first so that you can be honest with her. OR perhaps you've entered that you are a 'homeowner,' but- you really rent a run-down, filthy trailer that you sit in night after night, alone. If this is what you want, fine. You can become a hoarder all by yourself. But if you'd like to improve your situation and feel better about yourself, that will also help you in a relationship. Your self-esteem is important. These things take time to change, like jobs and places to live, but you may want to work on those first before you start dating.

❖ Anyone can improve their life at any step along the way. Start off with a small step. Is the trailer filthy? Get out the rags and window cleaner, and make your living space sparkling so that you feel good about where you're living while you check out the employment section.

❖ Instead of bellyaching about everything that went wrong in the last relationship that wasn't your fault, start making a list of things that would help you feel better about yourself.

❖ Most of all, be honest about where you are now. If you quit, be honest about it. If you never listened to her when the red flags started popping up all over the place, then be honest about that. If you started feeling resentful about the credit card spending, but said nothing, be honest about that. Communication is important. That was then and this is now. You can turn things around.

5 LIMO

Self-absorbed

PROBLEM:

We've all seen this man. I've always wondered if this type of man is even aware of how he is coming across. I would think this man's girlfriend would be reading this manual because he's so into himself and what he's doing and saying that he can't look past himself to see there might be other things going on and other people with feelings and ideas that may even be different than his own.

Should I really be addressing this part of the manual to her, so that she can pick it up and hand it to him? She is no doubt at her wit's end because when she talks to this type of man--well, that's just it... She doesn't talk. She listens. And listens. And listens. He is so caught up in what he's thinking and doing, he can't stop long enough to see that someone else is even in the room. He's semiconscious of it, but the way he comes across is that she's only there as his audience. It may not be his intention, but that's how it comes across.

Did you meet on a dating site and he seemed very interesting, so full of ideas and energy? Sure, he didn't ask you hardly anything about yourself, but you just put that down to his excitement over meeting someone new and wanting to present himself as a great guy. I mean, look at all he has going for him! Well, no, he didn't seem to pay attention when you got that promotion and, instead started talking about his own awesome experiences, but look what he's accomplished! His job is SO much more important than yours, right?

Then you met. There are so many good qualities about this guy that you start to feel selfish, wanting him to ask just one or two questions about you or your life. Or, my goodness, even your feelings! Imagine that! But he never does. When you try to get a word in, he jumps in, always with a smile, and finishes the conversation with his own interesting ideas or situations. He's pretty wonderful, right? He takes care of himself, has a lot of great ideas, is intelligent and has an important job. Your life almost pales in comparison. But, he can be helped! He's a great guy with lots of things to offer, but this is a relationship and you have just as much to offer. He may know that and that's why he's with you. He just isn't used to showing it or doesn't know how. He is smart enough to figure this out.

REPAIR STEPS:

❖ First, give him this manual and ask him very nicely to please read it. For you. For you both. Let him know how much you think of him and how this will help you both. He already has such an extensive library of knowledge that you just know he could help out with this relationship and help make it great for both of you.

❖ If he will agree to take a look at it, ask him what he thinks, specifically about this chapter. His ideas on it are important and that's why he'll read it.

❖ If he hasn't thrown it across the room yet, let him know that you would then like him to ask YOU what YOU think of this chapter.

❖ Use what each of you say as a starting point towards greater back and forth communication. *Use this manual!* That's it. It's a step.

❖ Make sure you let him know that you are with him because of all the wonderful qualities he has and what he has done with his life. A lot of times, this type of men are very high-achievers because they have an incredible ability to focus in order to achieve their goals. Unfortunately, that's great for jobs, etc., but in a relationship, both people must be the focus. Perhaps he has become so busy achieving his goals and working his plans, that he hasn't had time to see how this is affecting his relationships.

❖ Write a list down of things you know about each other. Have you been listening? Or has his non-stop chatter become an un-ending drone of information and you no longer pay attention?

❖ Has he been listening? Each of you write down things about yourself and see how much the other has been listening. If there are things missing that he doesn't know-then talk about those things.

❖ In your next conversation, make sure you have both given each other equal time to speak.

❖   He is not allowed to interrupt and neither are you--but this isn't about you, it's about him.

❖   This great guy you are with IS great, but so are you. If he challenges himself to focus on finding out what it is about you that makes you great and makes sure he tells you he knows what those things are, you will both feel more valued. He will gain a very happy, satisfied listener because he will put in efforts to be a good listener himself.

6 LEMON WITH A LIMO PAINT JOB

Made a mess of his life but thinks he's a prize

PROBLEM:

So, you've got this great job, wear a suit to work, and use the company picture to stick up on the dating website. You feel pretty good about yourself. You present well, you're articulate in your speech, and you can enter into intelligent conversations with ease. You don't have a drinking problem, you travel for business, and work out when you can.

Sounds perfect, doesn't it? You don't need to read this manual because you have it all together. Sure, you enter 'divorced' on the dating website, but you are friends and have learned so much from your ex, you say. You even get together on the holidays.

Well, no, you really don't own a house now but you're just biding your time to see where you want to settle first. Your life is perfect, really, and since you parted from your ex amicably, there were really no issues you had to work on. You just *grew apart*.

Yet, what exactly IS your job? If you travel for business, did that have anything at all to do with your last break up? What is your workout schedule? Five times a week? Really? Or is it really two when you can make it and can afford a membership? Have you really let go of your ex that is now your best friend or are you just hanging on because you have no idea what happened and think you can rekindle something? Who are actually at these holiday dinners and is it really her that isn't letting go? Is that why you go over to her place twice a week to 'fix' things or help her out with something?

Honesty is the key here. You come across as this man who has it all together and according to your initial statements, there's no reason at all that caused you to split up with your last SO. You just *grew apart*. Right. In other words, you were like the monkeys: you heard nothing, you saw nothing, and you said nothing. And you still aren't. You're presenting yourself as this healthy, together man, when you actually still don't have a clue what happened. It's not true that if you put forth a positive front that all the baggage of your past will disappear. It will rear its ugly head once again but it doesn't have to, if you can be honest. And you can. You don't have to float from one 'HAPPY' relationship with your best friend to another. Drop the front and be honest.

REPAIR STEPS:

❖ That's right, drop the front. The suit looks great, but it's just a cover. Put a picture up of you in a suit, sure! But stick that one up of you chilling out on the couch, too.

❖ When you are asked if you are a homeowner and you're not, say you're not. Period. If you have some money in the bank, great. But is it really enough to put down on a house or not? If it isn't, then don't insinuate that you're just waiting for the right reasons to find a place to settle. Don't give her the impression she will be the key to where you'll end up.

❖ If you really go to your ex's place twice a week to help her out, ask yourself what the real reason is. Be honest with yourself. If you're just a great guy and she's a quadriplegic and desperate for your help, then you get a star. However, people usually move on with their lives, so make sure you're doing it for the right reasons.

❖ How do you approach this with your potential dates? Do you cancel dates because your ex needs something and you just HAVE to help her? That's an automatic black mark if you do that. Next time, put your date first.

❖ Holidays at the ex's, complete with candles? Is it the whole family or just the two of you? Again, ask yourself what you're doing there and what, if you had your choice, would you rather be doing on Thanksgiving. If it's still to be there with her, then you're not ready to move on.

❖ How do you approach this with your potential dates? Does she ask you over for the holiday or do you ask her to come with you to your ex's? Believe me, this really happens! The ex is your best friend, right? And you want your new date to appreciate how wonderful she is, as well. No matter that you were with your ex for seven years and your new date for a month, right? Wrong. Start your own, new holiday traditions that you can share with your current date.

❖ Be realistic about where you are in life, right now. Be honest with people you meet about where you are in life right now. Don't say you're a business owner when you sell off your old clothes once a month on eBay.

❖ Do you find yourself making continual excuses that you're traveling and can't make dates? Check this out and see if this was also happening with your ex.

❖ Do you tell potential dates you drive a Jag, along with telling them you have an awesome job and your ex is your best friend, giving the impression you live some blessed life; then show up in a tattered twenty-year-old Jag with a crap paint job for your first date? Tell her you drive an old car if she asks. Don't just give the info you have a 'JAG'- giving the impression you're some fat cat (unless you are and that's your second car).

❖ Above all, be honest. You have an ex for a reason. If you were that great together, you'd still be together. Make a new life for yourself, be honest with how you portray yourself to potential dates or on dating websites. Don't gloss over what's really happening or who you really are. It will bite you in the end. You want her to like you for YOU, right? You're a great guy and don't need to hide it with a disguise.

7 STUNT CAR

Hidden pot smoker, alcoholic, transvestite, etc.

PROBLEM:

This section is for all you unusual men who have an added virtual sea of characteristics that make you unique. There are all different kinds of people out there and unless we're hurting ourselves or someone else, we all deserve a shot at happiness.

Where to start? There are so many in this category that, suffice it to say, any one of them can present additional challenges to a relationship. But if you hide any one of these initially, you're asking for it.

We can start with pot smoking. Not a big deal to you, right? It's just a plant and is no different than smoking a cigarette, only safer, right? If that is how you feel, then why hide it from her? Or, better yet, if she asks how much you smoke, why do you tell her once a month when you know it's every other night? Hiding things will make for big problems later on. Plan on it. How would you like to go test drive a car where the salesman hides some serious mechanical issues that don't show up in a short test drive?

Do you have a couple drinks every night? Maybe you don't drink for a week or two, then get totally wasted; then you're fine after that, and can be sober for weeks at a time. It's not my job to figure out if you're an alcoholic or not. You know who you are. But hiding how much you drink from her so that she has to be a detective to figure out why you appear drunk all the time, is not fair to her or to you.

Yes, women have pretty clothes. It rocks when you put them on. That's your choice to have any kind of paint job you choose, but if what you're after is more drama in your life, then let her find out by accident that this is one of your pleasures. Who wants to find out there's another layer of paint under there when we thought it was the original? Be honest. If feels much better to be accepted for who we are, doesn't it?

In short, if there is something about yourself that is unique, whatever that may be, it will be good for you and good for whatever relationship you end up having by being honest sooner rather than later. You can only deal with things honestly, once they are out on the table. You can like your whiskey, or your lacy panties, or having a joint. Or maybe you really aren't just 50 pounds overweight like you put on your dating profile. You're really are an insulin dependent diabetic with a foot amputation. Be honest about your unique situation. There's a lot to choose from in the lot. The trick is to find the best fit. And you won't find out who that is unless they know who YOU are.

REPAIR STEPS:

❖ As I said above, if you smoke pot every other night, then be honest about it. Just make sure she's not with the police if you're not in a medical marijuana state before you decide to bare your soul.

❖ There truly is someone for everyone. Why hide that you're a diabetic? Let her know your issue and when you do, she may even have some helpful ideas, if she truly cares for you. It's not cool to put a *few extra pounds* on your profile when the truth is the few extra pounds are only part of a larger issue. She'll figure it out, anyway, if you meet her for coffee and bring your insulin shots with you or if you're Skyping and she sees a zillion prescription bottles on the table next to you.

❖ There's nothing worse than finding women's lingerie in your boyfriend's house. It just leads to all those dreaded questions of *where did this come from?* This is a big deal, so let her know this is what you like, rather than have her find out when she sees you trying on her clothes or washing your bra.

❖ I'm not a counselor for alcoholics, so I won't go into the *don't date for a year* thing. You know who you are and the best thing you can do for her and for yourself in the long-run is to just be honest about your drinking. It's a lot to ask and denial just comes with this business, but if you ever want to lead a satisfying, healthy life, an important step is being honest. That old saying about how secrets keep you sick is correct. If you need frequent oil changes, it's best to be upfront about it.

❖ So, you haven't done your taxes for 10 years or have actually done them but cheated on them. No one wants to find this out after they've invested themselves in you, so it's a good idea to be honest on your taxes, but we know that might not happen, so the next best thing is to at least be honest with her about it all. I'm sure you have all the excuses ready such as, *Everyone does it in business*, or *My accountant never says a word* or (this is a good one), *This will never affect you*. Right. Let her make that decision. Don't you hate it when you go to buy a car and it cost way more than you thought it would?

❖ Do you have an oil leak? Okay, so you wear diapers. It happens. We all have issues. But again, you need to be honest. Don't let her find out you are incontinent by forking over the cash for an expensive hotel room, then telling her your ex had no problem with washing your diapers. This needs to be discussed before getting intimate.

❖ The Scammer from Nigeria. We all know YOU aren't going to be honest, but just in case you're reading this and have an actual conscience, can you just get a real job?

❖ Did you move the odometer back? You're 10 years older than you've entered into your profile because you're trying to attract a younger woman? You feel 10 years younger, right? And people tell you that you look SO much younger than your age! It's just plain rude to make up excuses why you're lying about your age, because that's what you're really doing. Be honest about your age and if you want someone a lot younger, then hold out for that person. But don't start out with a lie.

❖ You're 50 pounds heavier than any of your pictures. Okay, I know women do this too, but this is about you. Are you hoping she won't notice once you meet? She may be tactfully kind, sure; but you're starting out with a lie and believe me, she will be paying attention and looking for more lies after that one. Put up some current pictures if you're on a dating site and be proud of them. If you're working on your weight, then advertise the dents and be proud that you're working on your maintenance!

❖ If you are disabled and can't drive or are in a wheelchair, then you need love, too! You can hide it and tell her you just haven't seen the need for a car. Let her find out on the first date that you don't drive because you have to lie in the back seat because of your continual back surgery. OR you can just be upfront right from the beginning and you may find someone that wants you for YOU. Maybe you'll even find someone you can race wheelchairs with!

8 HEAD OF THE FLEET

The Manager

PROBLEM:

You're such a good Manager, Doctor, CEO, Real Estate Broker, Salesman... You've done well for yourself and know how to manage teams of people. The car lot is a smooth running operation. In fact, you're excellent at what you do and have received awards, professional recognition, and are held in high esteem by your colleagues. You have great ideas, great management skills, and know how to solve problems and run a team. If you're a doctor, maybe you're very proud of what you do and feel very special, indeed. God-like, almost. Maybe you're a therapist and already have all the answers, in which case I hope your girlfriend is reading this and can clue you in.

So, if you're a highly esteemed doctor, therapist, manager, broker or whatever- then why aren't your relationships working for you? It can't have anything to do with you, right? Well, because you're great at work doesn't necessarily translate into your relationship.

Is it hard for you to leave your business suit or lab coat at work where it belongs? A relationship cannot be managed like a business. It isn't a business, it is a relationship with two people involved. Sure, some people enjoy being managed and having all the decisions made for them. But if you're not a co-dependent or your relationships aren't working for you, then something is wrong.

Of course, you do have great ideas; you're intelligent and know exactly what would work in so many situations. You've come far in life and didn't get there by accident. You've worked hard and have a lot of experience knowing what works and what doesn't. You know people and how to manage them. But she doesn't need managing. She needs to be involved in the decision-making processes and listened to so that she will feel valued and like a needed part of the relationship.

REPAIR STEPS:

❖ When you get home from work and shed that suit, try hanging it in its own section of the closet, and think about it while you're doing it. Focus. Mentally take off your 'Manager' hat.

❖ First date: ask her where she would like to go and, while it's great to offer suggestions of your own, seriously consider going where she has suggested.

❖ Subsequent dates: rinse and repeat.

❖ If there is an issue in the relationship that you are both having trouble with, ask her opinion and resist the urge to 'solve the problem' and make up your own mind about how it should be dealt with.

❖ Do you deal with serious illnesses daily? That is to be commended, yes. You're very needed and valued. But are you so focused on what an awesome job you're doing that anything she says pales in comparison to your godlike stature? Try listening to her. Pay attention and actually respond to things she says.

❖ There's a huge issue that has come up in the relationship. Don't go off to your Board Room, make a decision on how to handle it, and then come back to her with your decision. Include her into the discussion. She may have some ideas that surprise you.

❖ Has she suggested that you both spend the holiday at a soup kitchen feeding the homeless, and your tradition has always been prime rib, gourmet trimmings and fine wine? There can be a compromise. You each have wonderful things to offer in a relationship that can help you both thrive and grow.

❖ Of course, you know what's best on the menu, but must you always order for her? Suggest some of the more tasty things on the menu and allow her to choose what she eats.

❖ Everyone knows you tip the valet, that you sniff your wine before drinking, and what to wear to a cocktail party. No, everyone doesn't know. Please, don't do your sniffing and turn your nose up at her because you are used to different things than she is. Help her to see how some things are done in your life, and encourage her to tell you about hers.

Look upon this as an opportunity to grow and expand. You might just learn something.

❖ In short- let go and let her in. Leave your suit, lab coat and power point presentations at the door.

9 TOW TRUCK B

Already hitched (aka married) and on the hunt

PROBLEM:

Seriously? You're married and looking for a date? Because of your marital status, you get the privilege of being last in this manual. Why? Not because I'm going to help you get a date, but because I'm going to help you figure out that you already have one. At home. Are you bored? Been married for a few years and wanting to add some zip into your life? Marriage going south and you can't figure out how to fix it? Your answer is to find another woman. Someone easier who won't question you on things, and who is happy with you just for being you. A smooth running engine.

In other words, someone who doesn't know you. That's so much easier, isn't it? Or are you just looking for a new make and model because you're tired of the *old* one? You've tried the dating sites that say 'married for married,' but somehow, have not been able to find a truly quality woman. (Imagine that!) Then you went on dating sites where, at first, you tried being honest about your marital status and that didn't work, either. So, this time you're trying something different, in hopes that this new method will expand your playing field. After all, you're a catch, right? Having a wife is just a technicality.

Let's say you're a doctor, have a lot going for you, a great personality, good looks (you've been told, of course), money (money always helps!), and don't forget the "People tell me I look ten years younger than my biological age!" BS... So you lead with all these wonderful qualities on a new dating site. You enter 'single' or 'divorced' for status. Just a little white lie, right? You were single once, so that did apply at one time in your life. Also, you *may* get divorced in the near future, who knows? You only mention yourself in your profile and diligently either cut your wife out of the pictures or submit ones with only yourself, preferably in your white coat. Yes! *Looking good!*

Hey, if she likes all the other things about you, how can she resist? (Rationalizations work great at this point!) You're off and running. You start putting your line out there (more like a barbed hook camouflaged in a juicy chocolate) and she bites! She's beautiful, appears intelligent, she's beautiful, likes to travel, she's beautiful . . . well, you get the picture. You write her these wonderful e-mails full of caring, humor and intelligence. You have a great job and interesting hobbies. You express interest in everything she does and says because you have an agenda here. You need to look good so that it will hide the surprise coming up for her. The e-mails go back and forth for a couple of weeks, just enough time to where you have decided you'd like to take it to the next step, and she is wondering if you are going to ask her out or if she should make a move. You ask her to dinner at a high-end restaurant. She is so beautiful when she shows up. Classy, intelligent, eyes sparkling in anticipation with hopes: she has died and gone to heaven! *Life is good!*

The dinner is amazing and so is she! You can tell she's interested in you and everything you do and say. This is working out. She is so caught up in you that you feel that when you casually mention you're married in between the main course and dessert that it won't matter at all. When she looks up in shock, you're amazed that this is even an issue, you tell her. You may not be married much longer or you say your wife doesn't understand you (of course), and you don't want to lose someone as wonderful as she is to this little wrinkle. In the meantime, can't you both get to know each other and establish how wonderful you are together and not waste precious time?

Well, no. Think again and think hard. Is this working, either? What is your goal here? Did you get married to find a short-term relationship? No? Would you like to challenge yourself to see if you can find fulfillment in the date you already have waiting for you at home?

REPAIR STEPS:

❖ You can try looking elsewhere over and over, but if it's a quality woman you're wanting, the first place to start is not on a dating site. It's at home. Dating sites can be great, but generally, they are for the single folks. (Unless you're on that one that busted you!) This isn't a manual to tell you how to snag that single woman to have dangling at your side. So stay off the internet while you work on your parts.

❖ Who really is this person you are with? Why did you get married in the first place? Try to go back and remember the things that first attracted you to her and write them down. Make a list. What are the positive qualities that drew you to her in the first place?

❖ Look at the situations that have happened since you've been married, and see what effect these had on you. Make a list, starting with the first one you can remember. In the beginning, when your cars were being manufactured to work together at the start of your marriage, you were attracted to each other for many reasons. Time and situations change people. People react to these situations, and that creates reactions in the other person and how you work together changes, too.

❖ Sit in a chair and imagine you are you. (The MARRIED you, not that dating you.) Focus. Then imagine she is sitting opposite you. Think of the difficulties you've had in the past and how you felt. How did you react? Did your engine just shut down? Did you raise your voice? Did you try to discuss it? How did she react? Did she raise her voice or try to discuss it, but she was crying so you then shut down? If you could go back to that moment, how would you have liked her to react? Just care about yourself for now.

❖ Then sit in a chair and imagine you are her with the real you sitting opposite her. Think again of these same difficulties you've both had in the past, and how she may have felt while she was busy reacting. Really get into this and FEEL how she may have felt. How did she react? Can you imagine why she may have reacted this way? How did you react in return and how do you think she would have wanted YOU to react? Care about her now. You both have to get the engines running smoothly and you can only work on yours.

❖ Is there a pattern to how you act when a difficult situation arises? Has it worked? If not, can you change that pattern?

❖ What are the good things happening in your life right now? Do certain things come up where you both have no trouble making them work? Why are they working?

❖ Have you lost your attraction for her? Do you know why? What are you looking for on a dating site that she isn't providing? Are there other things about her that someone else cannot provide? Something that would be hard to live without?

❖ You are still with her for a reason. Finding a substitute to provide some short-term pleasure is not addressing the issue of what is missing in your marriage.

❖ This is your challenge. Unless you're planning on divorcing, then get busy and get the tools out. It is the easy way out to look elsewhere and deceive another woman--in hopes of a short-term diversion from whatever issues you have currently in your marriage. Even if you don't deceive her in the beginning, you're deceiving yourself in the long run because eventually your hitch may come apart due to exactly what you're doing now, by dating on the side. It complicates the repair. This can be a fun challenge! Hey, you're not getting any younger, either, and there is a lot to be said for a woman who will put up with you! Find those awesome things that you've forgotten about her and get to work! You may not be alone in your disillusionment. Maybe she's secretly sick of you, too! You can turn this around and make life wonderful again!

10 GENERAL MAINTENANCE

Avoid broken signals, spare tires, failing battery, etc.

Broken Signals:

Have you sometimes wondered what she is even talking about? Or why she talks so long about the same thing, over and over and over? You may not be sending out clear signals or you may not be responding to hers in ways she can understand. Sometimes it's easier to understand signals that are nice and loving. It's when there's anger or distress involved that it becomes harder, and pushes all the buttons. When she brings something up, try not to shut down so that she can't even figure out what your signals mean. Look at everything--her eyes, how she is sitting, if she's gesturing while she's talking or if she's crying. Focus on the first thing she said and respond to that. If there seems to be a calmer atmosphere after you have responded to the first thing she said, that's a good thing. If the conversation gets more and more animated and agitated, then you may not have a clue, try asking her a question. Then ask her another one. If you feel like you know what she's saying, and then ask her if that's what it is. You may even be able to get through this today!

Spare Tires:

Are you 50 pounds overweight? You're been meaning to get to the repair shop for months now but just haven't gotten around to it? Or have you hidden it from her in pictures online? Do you think she will love you for you once she meets you and is in the presence of your awesome personality? Wrong. You've started off with a lie and who knows what the next lie will be. Do you really want to see her trying to hide the look of surprise from her face when she spots you at the coffee shop? It's best, once again, to be honest about who you are, so that she can have the correct information to figure out if she wants to have a second date.

Failing Battery:

When there is an issue in a relationship and she's upset, your battery shuts down, then your engine. Try to keep it from failing in the first place. If your initial reaction to something she has said that upsets you or you just don't understand it is to shut down, try to change that knee-jerk reaction from shutting down and driving away to staying in the room and talking. If you need to back yourself out for a short time and pull in later, then do that, but don't make it too long and let her know what you're doing before you race out of there. When you come back, jumpstart your battery and restart your engine and, although this may be tough, stick it out and communicate. Communication is the key. Keep the lines open.

Factory Recalls:

There are so many different things that can come up when we have a relationship. A lot of them are small issues that can be worked out if we both have the energy, knowledge, and determination to do that. Other ones are deal breakers, in which case, one of you gets sent back to the factory and you need to move on. Figure out what your deal breakers are and if they are valid. Can any of them be adjusted? Is your list so large that no one could ever meet your expectations? Are the things on your list really deal breakers or do they say more about your past? There are so many things that come up in the course of relationships that if you can whittle down that shopping list to a manageable amount of things you can't tolerate, you will be able to open yourself up for the many other things that may come up. Healthy relationships can happen, believe it or not! This isn't a 'me against her' situation. You are just separate people with different outlooks, perceptions, and pasts. Not wrong, just different. One car may have an incredible sound system, but the wheels on this new one are amazing! Embrace the differences, and try to realize and appreciate how they can enhance your relationship, not detract from it. This isn't a war.

START YOUR ENGINES!

Just like buying a new car, experiencing a relationship doesn't have to be hard or be called 'work.' It can be fun and easier than some make it out to be. You just have to know what part of your make and model is good for relationships, what might not be so good, and take the steps to fix those things that aren't. Just like fixing a used car, you can take steps to fix what is wrong, if you really want to. A lot of this is about being honest with yourself. You guys are great at fixing things, solving problems, and meeting challenges; and those qualities are a wonderful addition to any new or old make or model you might find. You can only maintain and repair yourself, though, then find out who you match with the best. Is your goal to have your own engine run smoothly so that you can attract another smooth-running engine to ride alongside you? You can do this and you can do it with a positive attitude. You are the key to your own happiness.

There is a sadness in failed relationships...

THE CAT AND THE OLD MAN

This story is about a cat and an old man. The cat was a very lovable, soft and furry cat that had never lived in a cozy house or ever received a steady meal or dependable warm pats on the head. The old man was a very kind and gentle old man with a good heart. He had fed an occasional animal before, but had never had any real pets of his own.

One day the kind wrinkled old man saw the soft furry cat while looking out his window. The cat looked hungry and since the old man had never had any special pets of his own, he set a small bowl of milk on his doorstep. The cat was very cautious but gradually he came up to the doorstep and gratefully lapped up the milk on the porch of the house. The warm sun held him as he filled himself with the cool milk. The dew glistened and shimmered on the grass in front of the house every day as the cat and the old man grew comfortable with each other. This went on for several weeks but the cat didn't feel totally happy, so one day the cat went up to the old man and rubbed up against his leg. Taken by surprise, the old man gave the cat a short pat on the head and the cat was happy.

Months went by. The old man was kind during this time, fed the cat and gave him occasional short pats on the head, but the cat still did not feel totally happy, so one night he ran into the house after the old man had fed him, jumped upon the old man's bed, and fell fast asleep. The old man was again taken by surprise but let the cat stay, since, after all, he was a kind old man and the cat was soft and lovable. The night was warm and caring as it surrounded the cozy house with its love.

Years went by and still the cat was not totally happy. The man fed the cat once a day, gave him short pats on the head, and had even wanted the cat to live with him, but the cat wanted more. The soft, furry cat wanted to be picked up in the wrinkled old man's large arms to be caressed and hugged. The cat asked for this in the only way he knew how and rubbed up against the old man's leg more often. The cat hissed when the old man ignored him. The old man said to the cat, "I am kind to you in one way, cat, but I cannot be kind to you in another." The cat did not rub up against the old man's leg as often and the old man started feeling unappreciated.

Many things happened to the cat and the old man during the years to come to cause the cat to hiss more often and the old man to become more impatient, but the cat and old man stayed together, nonetheless, and the warm sun still shone over the cozy house.

One day the old man became very ill, so ill the cat thought the old man might even die, and the cat was scared and the old man was scared. The cat and the old man up until now had had a relationship such that the old man would feed the cat once a day and the cat would rub his leg and the old man would give him a short pat on the head. Now the old man was tired and the cat was upset. The cat hissed more often and the old man was more impatient. The cat wanted more affection but the old man was ill and felt unappreciated. The cat tried again several times to rub up against the old man's leg, but the old man was very sick and impatient and told the cat to leave him alone. This became too much for the cat, so the hissing cat left the impatient old man to himself. The cat, in desperation, ran scared into the cold, dark alleyways in search of the warmth and love he so badly needed. The old man lay desolate in his sick and shriveled loneliness as the dark and warning thunderclouds flooded the roof of the chilled sad house with sorrowful raindrops.

A great deal of time passed in the dank clammy house that stood looking out upon the saturated grass, but after a while, the old man healed and was once again a kind old man. The cat did not hiss anymore and was once again soft and lovable. The old man spied the cat across the newly drying grass, called to the cat and showed him a bowl of milk on his doorstep. Since the cat was hungry, the cat gratefully lapped up the milk. Then the cat rubbed up against the old man's leg and the old man gave the cat two long pats on the head and picked him up into his large arms and caressed and hugged him. The sky was crystal clear in its brightness and again the cat felt the warmth soak through the thick fur coat on his back as the wrinkled old man stroked him. The cat was overjoyed that the old man was being so nice to him, but the cat was not totally happy, so the cat jumped down and started to run into the house, since he thought the old man was a kinder old man. The old man shut the door on the shivering house and said to the cat, "You have left this house, and even though I am kinder to you in one way now, I cannot be kind to you in another." The cat backed away a step.

The soft and furry cat, who had always wanted to be held, fed, and loved, and the kind, gentle, wrinkled old man who had always wanted a special pet to love him and be of comfort to him in his oldness, stood apprehensively on the doorstep waiting and wanting and questioning the reason for the unsettling weather.

by Becky Parquet

...but relationships don't have to be beyond repair.

ABOUT THE AUTHOR

Becky Parquet has used her experience, combined with her never-ending sense of humor and positive outlook on life to create this repair manual for men who are frustrated that their dating experiences are turning out to be harder than expected.

*Please feel free to visit my website at **beckyparquet.com** to contact me and share any experiences you've had or to offer feedback.*
I would love to hear from you!

www.ingramcontent.com/pod-product-compliance
Lightning Source LLC
Chambersburg PA
CBHW040346060426
42445CB00029B/16